Ten Steps To Speed Up Your Windows 7 Computer

A Step By Step Tutorial On How To Optimize Your Windows 7 Computer

Jorge Gonzalez

Learn Useful Computer Related Information On My Facebook Page at:

Random Computer Stuff

Why did I write this book?

I wrote this book with you in mind. We live in a technological age where most people own computers and use them on a daily basis. It is my intention to keep your systems running smoothly by showing you how to take care of your technological investments.

Why should you read this book?

You should read this book if you are interested in getting a better understanding of how your computer runs. You should also read this book if you are interested in making your windows 7 computer run at its optimum performance. If You are not comfortable doing a specific process then I would recommend that you skip it and do more research on the particular subject until you feel ready to try the process out. If you still do not feel confident in your skill level then it is always a good idea to seek out a professional. In following the below steps you agree that any process you do is of your own doing and you will not hold me liable for any damage that may incur. I believe in the work I do and attempt to be as close to being easily understood as possible. I would like to here your story's of success with this book and what it has done for you. Please take your time going through these areas and use your best judgment. This is not a race. You will understand this information over time and it will become second nature if studied and certain practices are put into play. Follow these steps to avoid confusion and do so with an open mind to maximize the experience this book has to offer. I believe this is knowledge everyone should possess in this technological world that we live in.

Table of Contents

Disk Cleanup

What is my disk?

Your disk is simply the area where you hold onto certain files on a hard drive.

Why should I clean my disk?

It is a good idea to clean your disk to speed up your computer. Erasing files you do not need takes away clutter that could be slowing down your system.

When is a good time to clean my disk?

You should clean your disk at least once a week in my opinion to keep your computer running in optimal condition.

How do I clean my disk?

- Left click on the windows button in the bottom left of the screen.

- Go to your windows search bar.
(Windows 7 users click start button then you will see the search bar.)

- Type in disk cleanup then left click disk cleanup

- If asked which drive pick your main hard drive. (example: C: or D: or E:)

- It will normally display your main hard drive first.

- Press the OK button

- Wait for scanning to finish.

- You will see boxes to the left with check marks. The ones that are checked leave them be.

If the temporary files folder is not checked then check it now.

NOTE:You can check the meaning of each area by left clicking once to highlight.

Temporary internet files should also be checked.

- Check the recycling bin box only if you are sure you want to delete the files in your recycling bin. Normally files you delete end up in the recycling bin.

- Once you have checked the boxes needed, go ahead and left click the OK button towards the bottom of this window.

- Windows will ask if you are sure you want to delete these files. Click delete files and your done.

Disk Defragmenter

What does it mean to defragment the disk?

 Your disc stores files in a way that can be cluttered and disorganized (Fragmented). When you think of something fragmented you think of something broken apart in pieces. Well it is similar in windows. To defragment is to put back together again. What that does for your computer is allows you to get to files faster as the disk has the files in one place and not scattered around on the hard drive. To put it simply it is a way of organizing the files on your computer.

Why should I defragment my disc?

 As Stated above it is good to defragment your disk because it will organize files and allow your computer to get processing done more efficiently.

When is a good time to defragment my disc?

 At least once a week would be good to optimize your disk and keep your processing for your computer quick.

How do I defragment my disc

- Go to start button and left click it.

- Go to your windows search bar.

- Type in disk defragmenter

- Left click on disk defragmenter.

- Look for your Main Hard drive.

(It is normally c: or the first option on top of the other options.)

- Left Click on your hard drive once.

- Once the hard drive is highlighted blue go ahead and left click the analyze button.

- Analyze will check to see the percentage of files on your computer are fragmented.

- Once complete you will see a number as a percentage on the drive you analyzed.
Example: C: 8/16/2016 4:34 PM(5% fragmented)

- Select the same drive again by left clicking on it, but this time click the defragment disc button.

This next part may take some time. This is the longest process of them all and is recommended as last process of optimization. As you wait you should see some information displayed.

Example: C: Running... pass 1 15% relocated
Just wait patiently. Sometimes it goes through the hard drive more than 6 times to complete this process. After it is done go to the next step

Power Settings

What are power settings?

Power settings allow you to make changes to the functionality of your display. They allow you to change when the computer goes to sleep or what kind of power usage the computer uses.

Why should I change my power settings?

You should change the power settings if you want to change the functionality of your settings for your display on your computer.

When is a good idea to change my power settings?

It is a good idea to change your power settings whenever you feel like changing how your computer behaves. Maybe you want the monitor to never turn off or maybe you don't want maximum brightness when your not plugged into the charger (for laptops).

How do I change my power settings?

- Go to your windows button and left click it

- Now go to the search bar.

- Type power options into the search bar and press enter.

- You should be on a page that says: Select a power plan

- Look for High performance and select it.

Note: If you do not see High performance as an option then look for show additional plans.

If you have followed all the steps I have given you so far your doing great and in no time your going to feel like your computer is so much more efficient then before. Take a minute and think about the above processes. Disk cleanup, Disk defragmenter, and changing the power settings are the start of optimization but we still have a few more things to do. Let us continue on this journey into your computer.

Uninstall Unnecessary Programs

This can be scary if you don't know what your doing. This process involves getting rid of programs you do not need taking up space on your computer. If you are unsure after going through this process then its OK to skip it. For everyone else let us continue. Understand that if you uninstall system programs from here you can mess up your computer badly. When searching in your program uninstaller be weary of programs that come from Microsoft and the maker of your computer. I will show you a picture of some of the files in my uninstaller to give you a better idea of what you are looking at.

In the next page you will see a picture of my uninstaller. Any item with a red dot next to it are things that were installed with my computer when I received it and will not be uninstalled. You will notice some of them have the name Microsoft corporation.

DO NOT uninstall Microsoft programs. Also you will see some other programs like realtec. Realtec are your speakers if you uninstall them than good luck listening to your music as realtec are the drivers for your audio devices. It isn't hard to research what these programs do just a quick google search will arm you with the knowledge you need. If you have minecraft and don't play it anymore, (unlikely) then you can delete that program. Those are the types of programs it is OK to uninstall. The programs you know of are the targets to uninstall. Ill show you a picture of what I'm talking about and then ill give you a breakdown of how to go uninstall programs. You may not have to uninstall any of these programs and can continue to the next step. Let me warn you that baddies like viruses and malware like to hide themselves in programs. One baddie I know of is chromium. Really nasty malware.

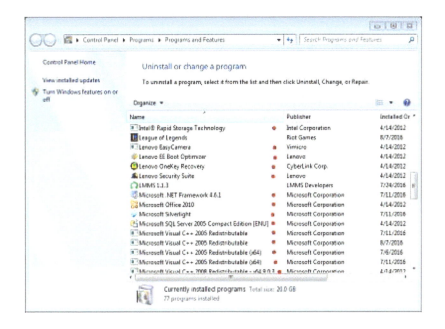

Uninstall Programs

- Go to your windows button and left click.

- Go to your windows search bar.

- Type in Control Panel.

- Left click control panel.

- Look for programs. Under programs left click on uninstall a program.

- Now you will be in the screen that you saw in the picture prior to reading this. This is where you will uninstall programs from.

- Left click one time on an item to select it.

- Once an item is selected just look towards the top for uninstall.

- Left click uninstall and follow any steps the uninstaller tells you to do to uninstall the program.

If a program refuses to uninstall then you may have a virus that is being pretty stubborn. In that case you may need to open your antivirus and scan your computer.

Another reason a program might not uninstall properly is a corrupted install file. Don't jump to conclusions too soon. If you have a problem your best bet is to google it. Somebody, somewhere, has had your problem remember that.

One of my favorite things to uninstall are toolbars that somehow end up on peoples computers without them knowing how.
Especially toolbars like the one called radio rage toolbar.
If you want to know more just google radio rage toolbar.

If you don't feel like there is any program worth uninstalling than go ahead and close out this uninstaller window and move onto the next area.

Change Bootup Programs

What is a bootup program?

A bootup program is simply a program that starts when you turn on the computer. An example of this is when you start your computer and get to the desktop after putting in your password (which is very important for protection reasons). As soon as you see all of your icons and desktop stuff your computer still doesn't respond fast. The reason for this is you have background processes that started when you turned on the computer. These processes can put your computer to a standstill for minutes while you wait for them all to load up before you can start using the computer efficiently.

Why would I want to change my bootup programs?

You should want to change your bootup programs to make your computer respond faster and more efficiently when started up.

When is a good time to change bootup programs?

Any time you install a new program into your computer it is a good idea to think about if you want that program to start as soon as you start your computer.

Remember this; Just because you stop the program from booting up when you start the computer; It does not mean it will effect the programs functionality.

The only difference you will see when you don't allow a program to start on boot is that you will have to manually start the program to get it processing.

Example: You disable iTunes from starting at boot or startup. Lets say you want to use iTunes. Just find the icon associated with iTunes, double click it, and then it will start working. When you run a program from boot it will be waiting for you to use when you start up the computer. I recommend turning a program on when you want to use it not when it wants to run.

WARNING! DO NOT DISABLE any Microsoft services. DO NOT DISABLE any manufacturer services unless you know what they are. Services you want to disable are ones you are familiar with. Only programs you are familiar with that you don't want starting when the computer starts should be disabled. Examples are: Ccleaner,Best buy Services, iTunes and so on. I would recommend you leave your antivirus on for bootup as you may forget to activate it during your computer use and may harm your computer by accident.

Here is a picture of what it should look like when you access the startup programs manager.

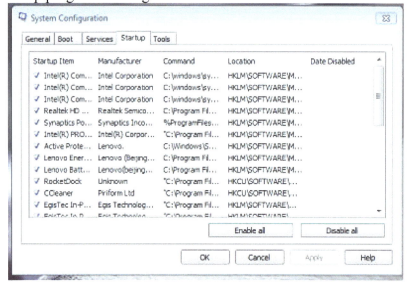

How do you change bootup programs?

- Go to your windows button and left click it once.

- Go to windows search bar and type in msconfig.

- Press enter and a menu should pop up called
system configuration.

- Look for the startup tab and left click it once.

- You will now see all the programs and processes that start with
your computer.

- From here you will uncheck any boxes of the programs/
processes you do not want to start when you turn your computer
on. I'll show you a list of the programs I use and some of them I
uncheck.

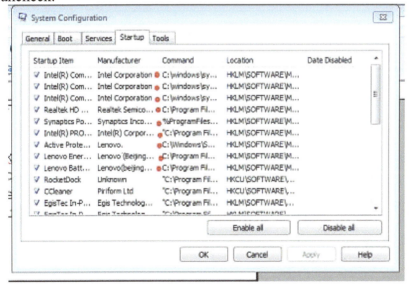

In this above screenshot you can see the box you should be
working in. Any of the processes that run on my computer that
belong from the manufacturers of the computer I do not turn off.
You can see the red dots I have put next to them.

This is where you use your better judgment to figure what you do not need to run on startup.

So now I'll show you a picture of the processes I do not allow to start on bootup.

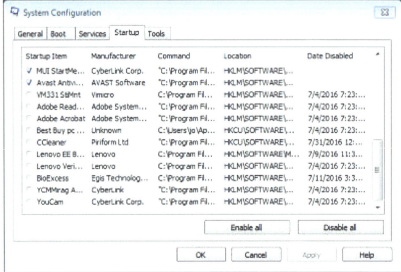

All of the above boxes I have unchecked are processes that will no longer auto start when I turn on the computer. Keep that in mind as you go through each one.

Example: I Disabled adobe reader because I don't need that to start with my computer; It does nothing for my computer other than allow me to read documents and does not effect the computer operation other than slowing it down. If I needed to read a document later on I can always start that process when I need it to work. Keep this mindset when you are choosing what you want to disable.

If you are ready now go ahead and look through the available programs and disable them as you see fit. You can also check each one in google by searching should I disable this on startup and you will get a yes or no depending on the type of program.

So you are ready to disable programs. To do so go ahead and uncheck the box of the program(s) you do not want to start when the computer is turned on. Now that you have the programs or processes selected go to the bottom right of this window and left click once on apply.

That is all you have to do to change your startup programs. This process will give you a noticeable difference in the speed in which your computer runs.

Change What Services are Running

What are services?

Services are what your computer uses to make all kinds of functions happen. This area is not for the feint hearted or unsure type of person. Just like the bootup window, and uninstall window, you should take care when going through what services you do not want to run. These services can be turned off but can harm the functionality of the computer if you turn off the wrong ones. If you decide to disable any of these services it is because you do not want them to run unless you force them to run yourself. Example: If you have iTunes disabled it will not do anything with your computer unless you go to your iTunes icon and force it to start. It is very similar to the bootup menu we just went over.

Why would I want to change my services?

You would want to change your services that are running in the case that you do not want that particular service to run. Its really that simple. This gives you full control and allows you to pick and choose what programs have permission to run at any given time on your computer.

When is a good time to change your services?

A good time to change your services is when you install a new program, as many programs will try to auto-start and run in the background which takes away from your speed and can hold your system back from its best performance.

How do you change your services?

- Go to windows button in the bottom left.

- Go to Your windows search bar and type in msconfig and press enter.

- It should bring up a window called system configuration.

- Now go to the services tab and left click the services tab if you are not currently on that tab.

- Look for a little box towards the bottom left of the window. It will say: Hide all microsoft services. This is here so that you don't accidentally disable a process that is needed for windows to run.

- Check the box that says Hide all microsoft services.

     You can now go and look at these services and pick and choose what you do not want to run and disable them. The areas with red dots next to them I would recommend you not disable. These processes deal with your computer directly through whatever CPU you are using. My computer uses Intel. Your computer may use something else just make sure like before, if you don't know what it is, do not mess with it.
Here is a picture

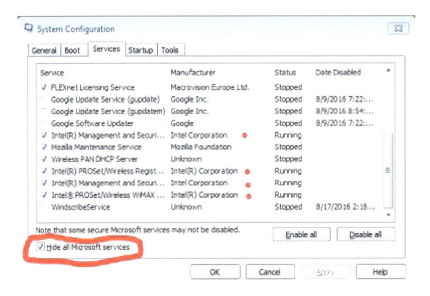

You will notice I turned the google update service off. Some would say this is a bad idea because if your software is outdated you are more prone to viruses and malware attacks. I have a certain time I like to update my browser so I keep it like this. It is entirely up to you, what you disable here. If you have Skype, I would disable it. If you have iTunes, I would disable it. If you want these programs to run then just go to where the file is located and turn the process on. Its really that simple. If you follow these guidelines you should have no problems and a more efficient computer.

By now you are very far into the process of speeding up your computer. You are close to finishing and may already be able to see a difference. An overview of what you should have accomplished by now is the following:

Clean your disk.

Defragment your hard drive.

Change power settings to high performance.

Uninstall programs you don't need or use.

Change what programs boot when you start computer.

Change what services are running on your computer.

Let's continue.

Change The Visual Effects On Your Computer

What are visual effects of a computer?

The visual effects of your computer are what you see visually when you look at your computer. You may not know this but you can make your computer look as standard as some of the very old versions of windows. An example of this would be the smooth edges you see when you look at an open window. They can be reverted back to squares (or sharp edges) like it used to be in older windows operating systems. These visual changes take more processing power to run and slow your computer down. You can change these visual functions to make your computer snappier and more responsive.

Why should I change the visual effects of my computer?

If you would like your computer to be faster at responding when you click an icon or you open a file it would be good to change these settings.

Is it a good idea to change the visual effects of my computer?

Yes it is a good idea to change the visual effects of your computer as it will speed up the processing power of your machine and enable your computer to be much more efficient.

How do I change the visual effects of my computer?

- Go to windows search bar and type in control panel and press enter.

- Left click on system and security. Then left Click on System. Now look to your left and left click on Advanced system settings. You should now be in a window called system properties. By default you should be in the advanced tab.

NOTE: You should be logged into an administrator account in order to be able to change these settings.

- In the advanced tab you should see Performance
- Left click on settings...

- The visual effects tab is what you are looking for. This is where you can change the visual effects of your computer. You have a few options to choose from. The options you should see are:

- Let Windows choose what is best for my computer

- adjust for best appearance

- adjust for best performance

- custom.

For this tutorial we will be attempting to customize without noticing too much visual difference. Some of these things I didn't even know were there until I looked really hard. Go ahead and choose the custom option. Copy the settings I have set in the picture on the next page.

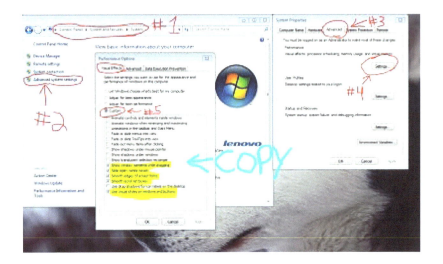

- What you are looking to accomplish is unchecking the boxes that are checked in the picture I have displayed for you.

- When finished copying the work I have done look towards the bottom of the window and you will see the apply button.

- Left click the apply button.

- Then Click the OK button and you have finished changing your windows visual effects.

You may or may not notice a difference.

　　If you don't then I don't blame you I didn't when I first changed the visual effects but it does make a difference in how your computer processing power is allocated.

　　What you should notice is a difference in the speed in which the programs are opening.

Add Virtual Ram To Your Computer

What is Virtual Ram?

Virtual ram is memory that your computer runs to make processes work. The more ram your computer can handle the faster your processes will work. Virtual ram is when you take a piece of your hard drive and allocate a page file which allows you to save that area of the hard drive to work as if it is physical ram.

Why is it a good idea to add virtual ram to my computer?

It is a good idea to add virtual ram to your computer to give it a boost in speed and make your computer run more efficiently.

When is it a good idea to add virtual ram to my computer?

It is a good idea to add any kind of ram to your computer at any time you can afford to because this makes your computer more reliable and efficient.

How do I add virtual ram to my computer?

-Go to your Start button and left click it once.

- Go to your windows search bar and type in control panel. Press enter.

- Once in control panel find system and security and left click on it.

- Next find system and left click on it.

- Look to your left for advanced system settings. Left click on Advanced system settings.

- You should be on the advanced tab in a window called system properties.

- Look for performance. Then look for the settings... button. Left click the settings button.

If you did the visual effects tutorial from before this window should look familiar to you.

- Now left click on the Advanced tab.

- You will see an area that is called Virtual Memory.

- Left click on the change button and a window called Virtual Memory will pop up. In this window follow my guidelines.

- The first thing you need to do Is look for the text that says recommended. Now look at this number and ask yourself is the recommended number bigger than currently allocated?
If it is then you can add more page files to the hard drive by following these steps.

- Uncheck Automatically manage paging file size for all drives

- Now go to custom size and left click it.

Now in the initial size box type in the recommended number. Do the same for maximum size. It should look something like the following picture when your done.

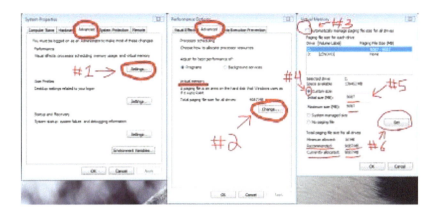

- If you notice I have a recommended number of 9087 MB.

- I put that same number in the boxes specified and left click on set to finish the process.

- Your computer will notify you to restart your computer in order to make these changes take place.

Go ahead and restart and wait. When your computer starts go back to see if these changes stuck. If they did congratulations. You just allocated page files to your hard drive in order to increase productivity to your processing and computer.

I know it sounds technical but it really isn't hard to understand and is a process anyone can do once you get used to it. Go ahead and pat yourself on the back you are learning how to optimize a windows 7 computer. Let us continue to the next Point of interest.

Turn Off Your Screen saver

What is a screen saver?

A screen saver is simply a window that pops up from inactivity with the computer. One type of screen saver can be different pictures of puppies cycling through after 1 minute of not using the computer.

Why should I turn off my screen saver?

A screen saver takes up valuable resources that can be allocated to processes that are more important to your speed of the computer your using.

When should I turn off my screen saver?

You should turn off your screen saver immediately if you want to optimize the speed in which your computer operates. A screen saver is not necessary as you can make the computer log off just by changing the settings in power options instead of pictures floating around after a few minutes.

How do I turn off my screen saver?

- Go to windows button and left click once.

- Go to windows search bar and type control panel. Then press enter.

- Look for appearance and personalization then left click on this option.

- Left click once on Personalization.

- Now look towards the bottom of the window and you should see

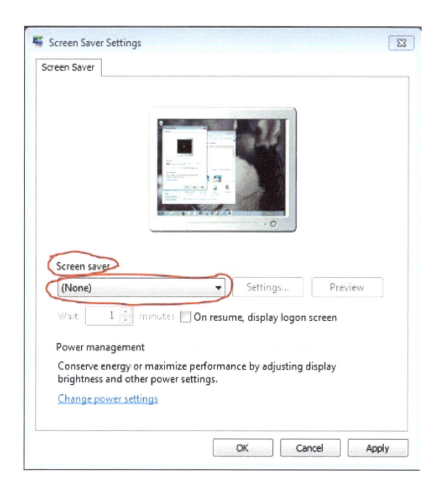

screen saver.

- Left click on screen saver.

- You should now be in a window called screen saver settings.

- Under screen saver look for a drop down box as shown in the picture in the previous page and highlight none. Left click on none.

Now click The apply button and then press the OK button and you are done here.

Install And Run Ccleaner

What is Ccleaner?

 Ccleaner is a computer program that allows you to clean up your computer files and change system settings in your computer.

Why should I install Ccleaner?

 It should be installed in case you don't want to go through all of the steps in this book and do all of the processes using the G.U.I. that Ccleaner provides.

When should I use Ccleaner?

 I would recommend using Ccleaner once a week to keep your computer running at maximum efficiency.

How do I install and use Ccleaner?

- Open up your web browser.

- Type in google.com and press enter.

- Now once in google type in the search bar ccleaner.

- You will see ccleaner in the top of the search results.
NOTE: Only go to https://www.piriform.com/ccleaner/download

- Go to ccleaner free and scroll down to the download button. click download.

- It should automatically start downloading.

- When it finishes downloading go to where you downloaded it from and double click the installer file(the file you just downloaded) to install it on your computer.

- Now follow the prompts to install it onto your computer.

- When it is installed and you open it go ahead and take a second to look around.

I'll briefly explain what each option does. In the next page you will see a picture of ccleaner once it has been opened. What I want you to notice first is cleaner and registry.

Cleaner is the same as disk clean. Registry is an added function that if you are not comfortable with computers I would not recommend messing with.

- Click on cleaner. Now if you click on analyze it will analyze your computer for files that have been checked off to your left.

Leave the boxes that are checked as they are if you don't know what your doing. Once you analyze you simply left click the Run Cleaner button on the bottom right to delete the files. Just follow the prompts after this.

The picture illustrated in the previous page is a numbered diagram of what it will look like as you go through this process.

The next picture will display the uninstall option for ccleaner which does the same function of what I showed you earlier of how to uninstall programs.

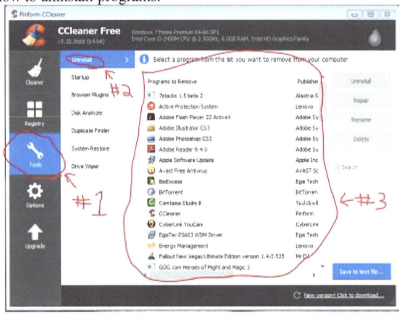

First left click once on tools. Then left click once on uninstall then select programs you want to uninstall and either uninstall, repair, rename or delete the items as you would like.

The next option you have with Ccleaner is startup which is the same process we did manually that stopped certain programs from starting on bootup. You can select any of these programs and disable them or enable them from here.

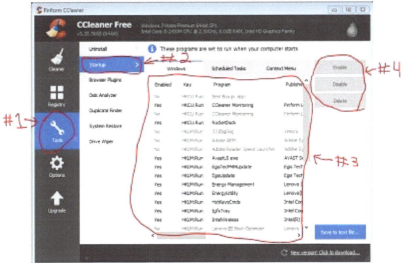

- Start by left clicking on tools.

- Then Click startup.

- After this choose the program you want to disable/ enable.

- Then finish by pressing the disable/ enable button.

We didn't talk much about browser functions but Ccleaner also handles those as well. Functions that the toolbars from your internet browser do can also be enabled or disabled just by following the steps in the next picture on the next page.

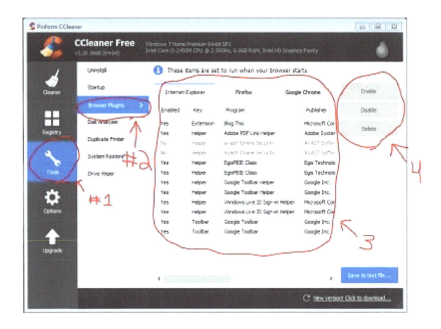

- First Left click on tools.

- Left click on Browser Plugins

- Left click once on the item you want to disable/ enable or delete.

- Now Simply Left click the buttons on the right to choose what you will do to the selected option.

- Wait for the process to complete and you have finished with this process.

Congratulations!

Now you have learned 10 things to optimize your computer and make it more efficient. If you have no viruses or malware in your computer it should respond faster and allow you to move more efficiently through your computer system. This book was meant to teach you how to do these things for yourself. Its like pressing the easy button. I did not start this journey to give you an easy button. I had the full intention of teaching you how to do things yourself so that you may feel a sense of accomplishment and become more familiar with your computer. I want you to feel like a professional.

The best way to learn something in my opinion is to learn it hands on and that is the reason for this book. I want to thank you for reading it and welcome you to read it over and over to perfect the skills in it. I am also open to any suggestions as I am not perfect and on this journey just as you are to be the best me that I can.

Please feel free to visit my Facebook page 'Random computer stuff' and let me know there if something may be wrong or something can be done better. If you liked the book and found it useful **please leave an honest review on amazon**. Thank you and enjoy your faster more reliable computer.

www.ingramcontent.com/pod-product-compliance
Lightning Source LLC
Chambersburg PA
CBHW041148050326
40689CB00001B/530